Ghost Hunting Equipment Guide

Written by
Lee Steer - Project-reveal Founder.

www.project-reveal.com

Thank you for choosing to view our guide on paranormal equipment's to date.

This is a great information source for any ghost hunter or paranormal investigator, anyone interested in making a paranormal investigations team themselves, as we will be showing you equipment's we use and know about, plus their faults and price.

Our aim is to make you understand a bit more about the equipment's, and make it easier for you to decide which equipment's you really need.

Throughout our guide we will tell you our hints and tips, regarding some of the best paranormal equipment's out there.

We at project-reveal are proud to present to you our

Ghost Hunting Equipment Guide 2013

Contents

Torches - Lighting

The first thing we would like to talk about is lighting, Lighting is one of the most important things you will need in an investigation for a number of reasons.
In order to investigate sightings of ghosts and spirits It's a must that you are able to see your environment, in some form.

Our suggestion of a lighting tool would be this 3 in 1 Lantern from RAC.
Price £20 - £40

In a paranormal group it is a good idea to have a spot light, Torch, and a lantern.
Spotlights are handy in big locations and outdoors to see far in the distance. A torch is good for your indoor investigations which are closed in, a lantern is ideal for area which you need to see a wide view of like caves tunnels etc.

UV Torch

UV stands for ultraviolet, which is a different light spectrum used in ghost hunting. Price £5 - £25

There is yet again a number of reasons why people use this, One of them would be to train the eye to see NEAR UV, as some believe that ghosts can lurk in different spectrums of light which we have trouble seeing like UV, and IR which stands for infrared.

Another reason would be to use with your Camcorder or digital flash camera which is able to see in the UV and IR spectrum.

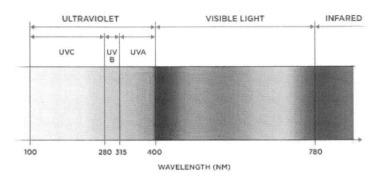

IR Torch - Illuminator

IR means infrared and is rather popular in the paranormal field, mainly to help your night vision cameras see a further field. i wouldn't recommend a small IR torch, as it will not make much difference to your camera's capability to see IR. I would recommend a IR illuminator which is in the style of a cctv camera. £5 - £80. Depending on IR distance.

If you purchase a 9v cctv clip adaptor, you can simply plug this into the cctv illuminator above and run it from a 9v battery instead of finding a power socket, next thing you would need to buy is a flash bracket or an hot shoe to connect this illuminator to your camcorder.

If you have Sony camcorders they sometimes have an intelligent hot shoe built in which enables you to equip Sony's IR Illuminators. Price £40 - £70.

Wildlife Camera's

Built-in 1-3/4"
viewing monitor

Mainly used for capturing photos of wildlife, and rare animals, they come in all different styles, and sizes. Most are small, easy to carry, and use SDHC card which you can put pictures straight onto your laptop from the card, they can take photos or video, on motion setting, or standard.

Why use this on ghost hunting?

Well the idea is to use this as a trigger object, the camera in the picture has two sensors, and once the sensors pick up movement the camera will take a picture using the IR lights above the sensors.

You can alter the sensitivity of the sensors, add time stamp, and moon phase,

Price around £90 – 180.

I would recommend using a wildlife camera in certain areas were you are not going to go, and then review any photos taken after investigation.

Strobe Light

Now if you are new to the paranormal scene you will be thinking why a strobe light?
Each day there is people like ourselves trying to find new and exciting methods of investigating the paranormal, and this is one of them. When you are in a nightclub, with all the strobes going off.. what do you notice? People move in frames because the strobe slows down your vision every time when it flashes. so the idea is that maybe just maybe! ghosts are moving that fast our eyes cannot see them, so this strobe will help slow down our vision and maybe see something paranormal?

Normally strobes are White Light, but in the paranormal world it is maybe a good idea to invest in different spectrum of light, UV, IR, You can simply buy infrared LED plastic, and place this over the glass on the strobe to block all visible white light, and lets through the UV and IR.
Price £10 - £40.

<u>Please note</u> this could be dangerous, to others who suffer with epilepsy so its best to check with everyone within your team first before using such equipment in your investigations.

IR Thermometers

Yet again a very popular piece of equipment out there on the market of paranormal investigations,
This Device monitors the temperature changes while on investigation. Pretty simple to use. With an lcd screen which tells you the reading, most thermometers comes with a IR light which takes readings of the object the light hits within a certain distance. This is ideal for taking peoples temperatures on investigations. To take an ambient room temperature its best to take off the IR beam so that way you're not getting a temperature of a single object. You can buy thermometers from £10 - £80.

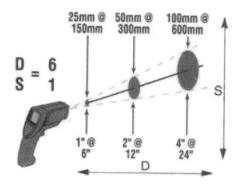

EVP Equipment

EVP stands for Electronic voice phenomena, and is probably the most common saying in ghost hunting. An EVP is where you do a recording on some device, and on the playback of the recording you hear something which wasn't there at the time of the recording.

If you hear something while doing a recording this would not be an EVP, this would be a voice phenomenon so it's important to not tag any Voice phenomena as an EVP on your write ups and etc.

Our advice on conducting EVPS would be to start the session with Time, Date, Location. Mention who's in the session, and list any interactions which you can currently hear. Try to have only two people speaking within the evp session where they take turns in asking questions allowing 10 - 15 seconds between each turn for a response. It is also important to tag any sounds heard which isn't paranormal in the recording to avoid false evps when reviewing.

Now to look at some EVP Equipment.

EVP Recorder (Dictaphone)

You can buy standard Dictaphones from a lot of places and they can vary from £15 - £80
Depending on the make and quality, The most popular would be Olympus in my opinion. The one in the picture above is model vn-2100PC.
It would be handy to find one which supports PC USB. For fast backup of files, like the one above.
Common issues with these Dictaphone's is when moving around you can sometimes cause wind like sounds on your recordings, so it's advised to place down your recorder to avoid this.

Extra Note: Do not place Dictaphone's next to EMF meters, as they have a magnets inside the records which the EMF meters will pick up on.

Zoom h2

This is a professional recorder which captures true stereo, with a total of 4 mic pickups which is capable of recording the environment by 360 Degrees which captures true stereo sounds, which allows you to toggle through different mic pickups to be activated. Used for podcasts and radio work, and music recording.

The standard Dictaphones recorder 80 Degrees or smaller, which has less chance of recording true sounds of an environment. This device has many features to many to list. This device can also be attached to a tripod

A good thing about these professional recorders is that it supports live audio which can be used for REAL TIME evp recordings. This is where you hear EVPS live without playing back the device. When you here LIVE evps its best to note down the time you heard the EVP for easy review when you transfer the evp file. The thing to note down is before classing it as an EVP you must verify that no one else heard the sound but you, a way around this would be for someone to Tag sounds as they happen during investigation, so if they said a Car going past, and you heard a car going past you know it isn't an EVP.

Price: £90 - £130

Abit more technical

If you want to push evp to the next limit you can always buy a wireless sound transmitter or a large cable jack and run the zoom h2 direct to your laptop in software Audacity or Digital Wave Pad. this will allow you to view the spikes of the EVP Recording and capture a true ambiance of the room. It's best to have someone sit and monitor the EVP coming through the line making logs so then it's twice as easy to pull off the EVP.

EFP

The EFP Stands for EVP Field Processor
This is a black shaped box with a vu bar graph. the device plugs into a LIVE audio EVP recorder, which you then plug ear phones into the Head phone socket of the EFP.

This device amplifies the ambiance of the recording your doing, and transmits it to your head phones, A tip would be to buy a Jack cable, and plug it into the head phones socket, which leads to another voice record, That way you are recording the ambience of which the machine amplifies.

You can set the White noise tone, by the dial on the left hand side, which moves the VU chart up and down, the best thing to do is level it to the RED, Middle, then you can watch for any spikes on the VU chart as well as listen. **Price: £50 – 100**

EMF Meters

EMF stands for Electromagnetic field, and this term is used a lot in paranormal investigations .

It is believed out there that ghosts, spirits consist of emf fields, so people use EMF meters to try and prove their existence, However there is many things which can affect these meters such as mobile phones, Wifi, Electronics in general. It is normally pretty easy to find the natural causes which affect the meter, 1 in around 10 locations we will find odd EMF reading which we couldn't pin point to something within the place in question.

K2 Meter

The most common ghost hunting EMF meter is the k2 meter with 5 lights at the top of the device which tells you field strength. There is 4 Version of this meter, with every new version there is a small perk. The price range is **£35 – £80** Depending on the version.

<u>Version one:</u> The typical meter with push in on / off, which you need to keep pressed in for it to work. This is a fault because it is so easy to lose grip and have false readings.

<u>Version two:</u> Same as above but you no longer need to keep button pressed in

<u>Version Three</u>

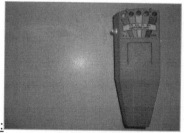

Same as above but with a red LED attached to the side of the meter,

<u>Version Four (Rare)</u>

Same as Version two with a Input jack built into the base of the unit, this is to plug in a speaker, Or Voice recorder via a jack, or simply plug in headphones to listen to the EMF fields as they happen

K2 Meter - Other notes: All these meters act the same when low battery, the first LED will be a bit dim, and will flicker the Full readings every now and then, until the battery is changed, I would recommend a new battery every investigation to avoid false readings. Also Version 4 info sheet tells you to use a speaker or a voice recorder plugged into the device. This may give false readings also since both have magnets in them which will affect the k2 meter when moving them around.

ELF Zone Meter

Elf zone meter is a simple meter with 3 lights built into the base. A Solid build, fast movement normally does affect most meters, but with this meter it doesn't. However the sensitivity on this meter isn't great. But I would recommend if you are just starting up since it's only about **£10 – £15.00.**
Green (safe) Orange (caution) Red (Danger)

Gauss Master

Yet again another popular meter out there on the field, fitted with a number scale which tells you the reading, with a high and normal sensitivity setting. When a high reading occurs it will sound a buzzer. This meter is very sensitive. And normally costs around **£20 – £30**

<u>Other notes</u>: Faults of this meter is that sometimes the buzzer can keep on, when the reading has in fact gone, also fast movement can affect the meter. So it's important to walk slow..

Electrosmog – (Esmog)

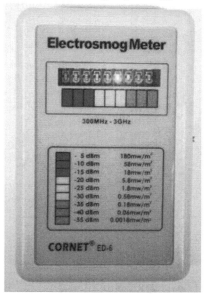

In my opinion a cheaper Version of the K2 meter which is more sensitive. This is a square unit, with on and off switch at the side, with a bar graph of Lights along a scale of numbers. There is two version of this device, which the only difference is a sound buzzer. The price of this device is £20 – £25 which is very cost effective and well worth the investment for any group.

EMF Tester

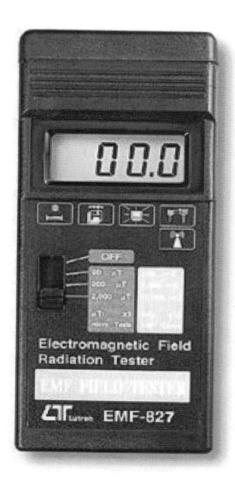

A square unite with a round probe attached to it, which is the sensor for the EMF fields. There are 3 settings on this device, with a LCD screen which tells you the Field reading. This device is great for scientific data readings for your team. We cannot spot any faults with this device and normally costs around **£45 - £60**

Tri field meter

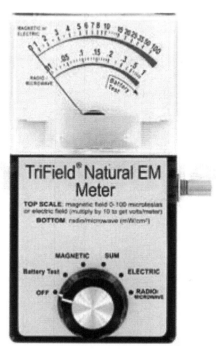

This is a rather expensive piece of equipment with 4 settings, with a Needle gauge graph, which is very sensitive, this meter is so sensitive it can detect the earths own magnetic field.

Settings are: Battery Test – Electric – Magnetic – Ion Sum.

Each field is used for all different reasons – to find natural fields which could in fact cause activity's, Ion Sum is both electric and magnetic fields it can detect.

Extra notes: The theory out there is that ghosts are made up of Electrostatic / microwaves, if you were a move a magnet it would turn into an Electrostatic field instead of magnetic. So in principle if a ghost is real and still "not moving" it would be a magnetic field.

Cell Censor

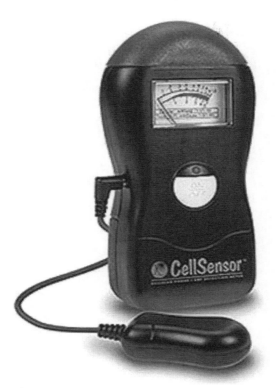

Yet again another meter similar to the gauss master, this is a nice style meter with a needle Gauge which tells you the readings of the fields. Also has a high and normal setting for sensitivity, comes with a thin wire probe which fits into the side of the meter. When EMF's fields reach a high level a red light appear with a buzzer letting you know there is a high reading. This normally costs around £25.00 - £35.00.

<u>Other notes</u>: The probe is very sensitive to movement any sudden movement will result in the Red light coming on and the Buzzer. It is best to keep a steady hand at all times with this device. Also when battery is low, turning on the machine will sound drained.

Moditronic Ramsey

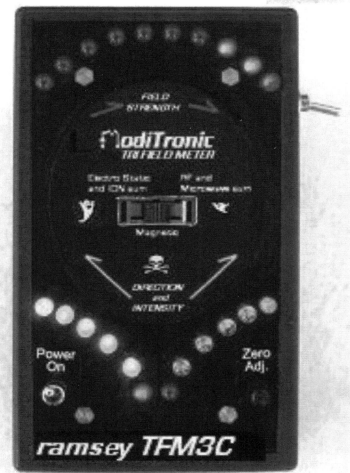

Most expensive EMF – Tri Field meter out there, this current model isn't in production anymore and is now a rare item., but you can find a downgraded version of the meter, which you will need to build yourself as a kit.

Like the Tri Field meter we talked about before this monitors, Electrostatic, Magnetic, and ION Sum. But without the battery test option, however this meter does have some handy perks...

There is a row of light at the top of the unit base, which a red, and they indicate the field strength. In the middle of the meter there 2 row of LEDS which lead in an arch like pattern, one leading to the left and the other to the right. This tells you the direction of the reading in question so it is better to pinpoint where the reading is coming from.

Another great thing about this meter is that it has the ability to register peoples own Electrostatic field By touching the Meter place on the base, this will then cancel out your own ES reading effecting the meter. If you are in an area which has a slight EMF field you can cancel that out as well with the zero adjustment nozzle on the unit base, this can be sometimes tricky.

Other notes: This is a great piece of equipment but can be to fussy to deal with, every time you start the meter you will need to zero adjust with the nozzle so just the 2 red lights are on. This can be very tricky at times.

Full Spectrum Camera

Here is a Camcorder / Camera which can see the FULL SPECTRUM.
UV: Ultraviolet - White light, and IR: Infrared

Used in daylight and night-time "an IR light source is needed to see in total darkness"

There are many versions of full spectrum cameras, Andy from Infraready can tailor to your needs, and budget
I would suggest going to www.infraready.co.uk

Franks Box

A franks box is also known as a "ghost box"
Which is simply a radio which scans the AM or FM radio wave bands
and never stops on a channel, it just keeps sweeping through the
channels from start to finish.

It is believed that ghosts and spirits can talk through such a device, in
America people have held sessions and charged the public "similar to a
clairvoyance night" were people ask questions to the box in turns, and
see if they get a message from their loved ones.

These are pretty expensive on the market at the moment,
£50 - 100
There is several versions of a franks box, with a simple ebay search you
will find them.

-

<u>Other notes</u>: Mainly used as a spiritual tool, some scientific teams do
use these devices but, the words that come through is not 100%
evidence of ghosts, as it could be just pot luck,

GEO Phone

Here we have a strange looking device which may look like something from the film ghost busters.
This device is a vibration censor, the stronger the vibration the more lights which light up. Some devices have a sensitivity dial at the top so you can make it more sensitive, or less sensitive.

The idea is to use this, as a trigger object on investigations, with a camcorder pointing towards it, Or during an EVP session, while everyone is standing still, you ask the spirits to make a bang, this device would then tell you if it picks up any vibrations around the device, some have sound as well, which alerts you.

The price varies from £30 - £80, depending on the version you buy. Some just have sound, some just have leds, and some have both.

Beam Barriers

 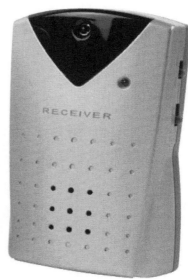

An often used piece of equipment normally used in a locked off room, where there is activity of a spirit walking past the hallway, room, etc.. You line up the two devices pointing at each other, at both ends of the room or hallway; if something breaks the beam the barriers will sound a loud buzzer, which will alert you that the beam has been broken.

These are pretty loud, that loud they can get annoying if they are purposely tripped by yourself, so it's advised to put them somewhere away from where you will be. Its also advised to have some some of video recorder or CCTV camera watching the device, to prove no one walks past.

These can be bought at around **£5 - £20**

Humidity Meter

Not often used on paranormal investigations, but its something what we use on investigations, A humidity meter measures the amount of water droplets in the air.

The idea is to use this device as a debunking tool, Or a trigger object. (Asking spirits to affect the meter)

For example if a member of your team gets an ODD MIST picture, which they think isn't their own breath, then the idea would be to use this meter and get a % on humidity, if the humidity is above 80% then it is very possible to photograph the picture.

Price: £10 - £100

Data Logger

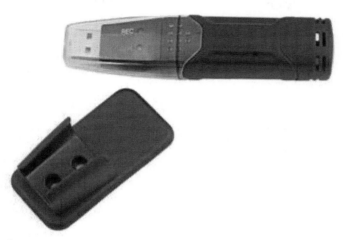

A data logger is a small object which looks like a usb flash memory stick,
This device monitors and logs Temperature and Humidity at the same
time within the time intervals your set via your laptop. Once set you
can remove from your laptop, and place anywhere you like within the
location to log the temperature and humidity every 10 mins, or so.

Once finished you plug the data logger into your laptop and choose the
time you want to view a report from and to.
It will look something like this.

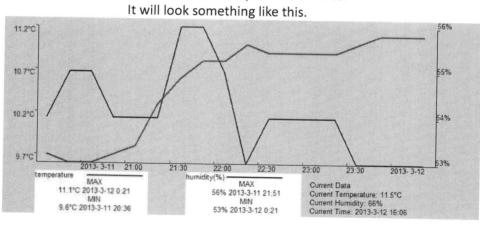

Prices are: £30 - £60
EM POD / PUMP

An em pump, or pod is a small device which simply pumps Electro Magnetic fields into the air, around the device, It is believed that ghosts and spirits feed of energy, so many people and teams have reported equipment drainage of their batteries, and swore blind they was charged, having an EM Pump around is meant to help save batteries and also give the spirits energy to do something if they are truly around.

In my personal opinion these devices haven't done anything for us..

Prices are: **£20 - £60.**

Parascope

8 CHANNEL
TRIBO ELECTRIC
FIELD METER

This is a funky looking device, which is basically an Electro Static field meter. "Not an EMF meter" This device is very sensitive, it can detect your own electro static field.

The main idea is to use this object as a trigger object.

The tubes show the direct of the field, and the movement.
A mixture of colours, from green, orange, yellow, red, which is very bright when the lights are off, which is great for any camera with or without night shot.

The device takes 4 AA batteries, and is bought from Paranologies
www.paranologies.com

IR SHADOW DETECTOR

A device you use with a laser grid pen, or White light.
Setup the item in a room; place a laser grid next to the device.
When a shadow appears in the laser grid, the device will beep, and a
light will show, If you use the device with the lights on, it will also
detect shadows "black shadows"

With the lights out you will need a Light source to use the item.
With the lights on, you can just place the item anywhere, and see if it
will pick up on any shadows.
Price $50

You can buy this device from
http://www.apparition-tech.com

Sound Level Meter

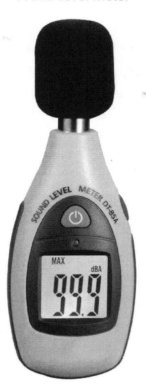

A sound level meter isn't used that often on an investigations either, mainly used by scientific teams to take base readings of ambient Sound, on which we can't hear, less than 20hz, these devices can listen way beyond that, sadly you can't plug head phones into the device or record in any way, it's just a chart of numbers from 0 to 100, you should really never get a 0 reading, as there is always some ambient noise.

It is possible to use the meter in your evp sessions, as some devices have a back light so you can read the numbers in the dark, The idea is that you could ask questions, and watch for any spikes in sound after you asked the question.

Price: £7 - £40

Laser Grid

A laser grid is something which was introduced into the paranormal field at around 2010, from TV shows, in the paranormal field.

It is a Laser pen, but it has an attachment at the end which splits the laser into 1000s of little dots, which you can adjust, size and quantity by turning the cap.

The idea is to use this with a Camcorder or Camera and take pictures of the grid, to see if any objects images show up in the grid, IF something was to walk in the grid you would see the green dots come close.. and see a shadow on the grid from the camcorder.

Price £5 - £35

CCTV Equipment
USB DVR

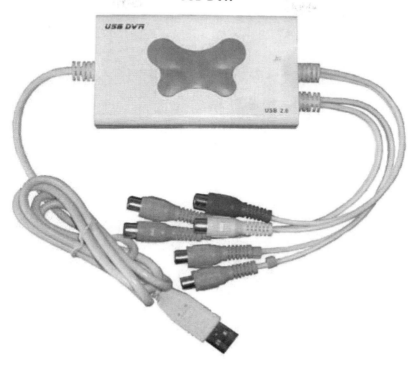

You can get 1 channel or 4 channel usb dvr's which plug into your laptop and turns it into a CCTV system. Plug the DVR into the USB socket on the laptop, then You plug your cctv cameras into the yellow sockets on the DVR, Open the software which comes with your DVR, and hit record.

You can buy illuminators, and all different type of CCTV Camera's

Price £8 - £60.
Cheapest place is ebay!

Thermal Imager

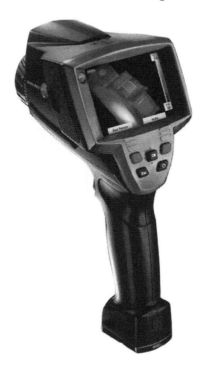

This is the Holy Grail for paranormal investigators, more of a dream piece of equipment; the thermal imager is used to identify hot and cold spots, of surfaces. These are not made to spot mid-air temperature changes.

A thing to remember is the smaller budget cameras just take pictures, but you can purchase a DVR for them to record, a simple ebay search for thermal imager, and you will find both Camera's and DVRS

The Pendulum

A low budget spiritual tool for paranormal investigations, mainly for the spiritual teams, the idea is to keep your hand as still as possible and ask if there is any spirits to come forward and move the Pendulum, Tell them to move the pendulum Clockwise for Yes, Anti clockwise for no.

Price : £1 - £5

Other Notes: To make this a scientific experiment, purchase a Jewellery stand for chains, ask people to touch the bottom of the stand, this eliminates movement caused by holding the pendulum, Its best to find a metal stand, to conduct your energy.

3D Full Spectrum Camera
(or standard 3D Camera)

Yet again this piece of equipment isn't used much out there on the field, I see a 3d camera, as a useful tool for spiritual and scientific investigators, because it enables you to see were about the ghostly apparitions are within the picture on which you may capture.

On a standard Camera "non 3d" you can always tell how far away an object is, or or close something is. Using a 3d camera gives you an actual visual on where things are, which may in fact help you de bunk pictures.

If you would like to buy a 3d Full Spectrum Contact Andy at
www.Infraready.co.uk

Van Der Graaf

The Van Der graaf is an odd looking scientific piece of equipment not often used on investigations, it's like a HUGE EM PUMP.

The device makes big amounts of Electrostatic, which comes from the belt, into the Metal dome; if you were to touch the dome you would get a nasty shock.

2 Reasons on why you would use this device is <u>to flood a room with electro static</u>, and lock off a camera in the room to see if anything happens, "totally lock the room down, close all doors, and don't go in until you want to turn the machine off"
The other reason would be to do a <u>Van der Graaf Séance.</u>
A couple of people sitting around the van der graaf, 2 people touching the metal dome at each end, all linking hands, so you're making a circle including the Van Der graaf, then get someone out of the circle to turn the machine on.
The idea is that it is meant to help spirits do something or effect you, but a thing to remember is that Positive energy has a negative effect on the body, making you feel sick, feel like your been touched and etc.
Price: £150 - £500

Wireless EVP

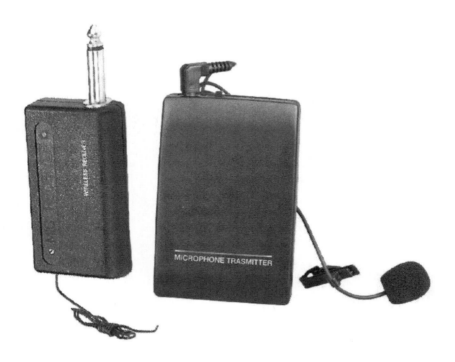

This item is a Wireless Mic, and a Receiver which plugs into the laptop's Mic socket. Simply place the Mic in a room on what you want to monitor, Turn on the Receiver plug it into the laptop,
Open Audacity "search Google for Audacity download" which is an audio program, which you will listen to the live steam of the EVP you left in the room upstairs.

Price: £8 - £40

Here we have another edition from paranologies, This is yet again
another cool looking funky design.
This device shows ambient temperature change in the style of Blue for
Cold, and RED for hot,

This device is intended to be used as a trigger object, so asking spirits
to walk past the device and etc, to see if there are any temperature
changes, the good thing about this item is yet again it is easy to see in
the dark! So that means your camcorders and etc will have no trouble
seeing them, when they get interfered with.

Price: £50 - £80
www.paranologies.com

Thank you
Well that's it for Issue 1,
Of our ghost Hunting Equipment Guide

We hope we have gave you many ideas on what you want to do within
your own team and what you want to invest your money into!

I would like to thank all teams and people involved in making this book
possible.

We will be scouting for new equipment's to feature in Issue 2 of our
book, please email asteer8@aol.com to ask about advertising your
products in our book to our readers.

Please don't forget to visit our website
http://www.project-reveal.com

Like our Facebook
http://www.facebook.com/projectreveal

Printed in Great Britain
by Amazon